Ink and E1

Book Two

CW00865736

...

SKETCHING SOUND

FOR THE APRIL HAGERS OF THE WORLD

ROCK -N- RAMBLE

THE SUNDOWN (GONE GREY)

CONSECRATING FLAME

A WINTER WITH NO CROWS

VERBATIM

KISS THE RAIN

WALTER MITTY'S REBUTTAL

...

Poetry
by:
Shane Windham

Cover art by C.D. Coleman.

ISBN 978-1475111798
All Poetry is the Copyright © of Shane Windham (2012). All Rights Reserved.

-CONTENTS-

CHAPTER ONE
-Sketching Sound-

Blue Hollow

...

Adept Perception

...

Almost Strangers

...

Two Weeks Too Late

...

The Legend of the Moon Goddess:
A Cancerian Tale

...

I Don't Know a Thing about Love

...

Pretty Scars

...

Battle Cry of the Unjust Sunset

...

Cut By the Blue

...

Underwater Rainstorms

...

Middle Earth Souls

...

Careworn Cloudbursts

Blue Hollow

I walk empty feet blind
every night, beneath the trees;
rarely aware of where I am,
and never knowing where I'm going
Growing ever more afraid
of a bullet behind the shade,
out to take more than my name when it comes
And these oaks, they don't glow
How I wish they would though;
as does every other moonlight child
that's trampling these wooded winds wild
...But no...
They shake, they sag,
they rattle, they haunt
Moving my pulse amid a quiet frenzy;
past every mailbox full of memories
that the dark (I'm aware) will never share
I'm yet a stranger within a burden,
but I dare not make its acquaintance
For you're only lost when you stop,
and I have a home to get to
So my sightless feet wander on;
float along mid-moon's blue hollow
Till I'm safe in the arms of a fireside;
finding ease in my lover's warm heart

Adept Perception

There are paths into the shadows
which condemn a man to darkness,
but we trek them for a reason
Reason being: all challenges end
We grow greater
All trails end, or (at the least) diverge
And, when that happens,
we may (with any luck) come to realize
that no man finds himself
within a mirrored reflection;
before the light which traps his intent
For among the falling shade, dreams are born,
and belief in that second star to the right
(so, oh, so bright beneath
a moonbeam of clarity)
reappears to eyes of ice and steel
It is there you'll hear the bards playing,
humbly, the tunes of a majestic rebirth
The choice then being between
that of a free heart and a popular thought,
once this change befalls his footpath
Shall he step back into the light,
or follow that star... straight on 'til morning?

Almost Strangers

I would like to know her better,
but we can't find the time
I spend years on these details,
yet the words still don't rhyme
Nothing is sacred between us,
unless you consider what goes unknown
Misplacing what should be between us;
forever hanging up the phone
Patiently awaiting a gentle phrase,
but never admitting what we feel
Always refusing to see it;
pretending there's some other way to heal
We discuss the past like a pun,
when it was warm with hugs and love
We drift apart, and lose the other,
but she remains the one I dream of
And this delicate thread which holds us together
deserves to be made of gold
But I fear, without more courage,
we'll soon be but memories; growing old

Two Weeks Too Late

It was only a sock which she bruised
as her voice fell down the stairs
Her arm was torn,
but our tongues were to touch
And by her lips
my safe haven was taken
beyond her palm-reading eyes
Her tears were warm,
though she never cried them
Our heartbeats collided,
and they matched
Oh, so strong was the morning,
where once had been only a sunset
upon our uneven blue-beat dream
Right then and there, I saw her as she
she swelled within some unreasonable sadness,
and yet I thought it was wonderful
to live amid her perception;
to breathe the night in
(the smoke, and the stars)
And in my mouth
lay every tear she freed
when the time finally came to cry;
when she first became everything
I already knew she had the ability to be
...Surely some piece of me must still orbit
that star-sized heart she owns...
She was the only blossom I saw bloom in my youth;
the only petals for which I knew birth
and (far ahead of time) mourned death
Just yesterday she was here;
today I'm not so sure,
and tomorrow's pretty clear
For all of my time is spent with her,
and even now that she's gone,
my heart tells me to love her
Two weeks too late
Today comes too soon,
and my heart's an empty picture frame

The Legend of the Moon Goddess:
A Cancerian Tale

A woman walks alone
within the dark craters of the moon
Her eyes glint without pupils,
and her toes glide through the cold rocks
She grins blankly,
and twirls her powerless wand;
her body bathed in liquid silver
The silver, coated in beads of sugar
You're tempted to drink her flesh,
but wouldn't live to tell of her taste
She wears a see-through sheet of sky
which flows about her body;
drifting carelessly in the literal space behind her
She casts her spells upon gravity,
and takes credit for turning each tide
She gave the world her secrets
for the price of a smile;
equal parts seduction and insanity
She alters the way we imagine;
drowning our dreams in a peaceful fear
Leaving us spellbound and weeping
in a flood of silence

I Don't Know a Thing about Love

You asked me to carry your picture,
and to tell the world you were mine
But only so the world would leave you alone
And I ended up lonely when you wound up in love

Still, I was the worst kind of friend
-the one who wants more and just won't confess
You can beat him at hearts, but he'll takes yours
to hold like a prize
that's only use is taking up space
in that empty place he's afraid to acknowledge

Too proud to admit he's unsure how love works
When the obvious enemy is the thought itself
For love doesn't equate like a dotted line
You can't compute what's unconditional

And I didn't start thinking to stop thinking
until I ran out of numbers...
By the time I had no answers
all we had were reveries

But I still carry that picture
And now that you carry the heart
that I finally understand isn't understood,
I just wish I were confused again

For if that's all it would take to make
you plus me equal we, I'd let the world see
that I don't know a thing about love
Because I'd just be happy to have it

Pretty Scars

I cling so tightly to the days I saw my father cry,
to remind myself that every cold heart still feels the chill
My love was beyond reluctant to see that you'd gone
But, with time, I stopped thinking I was going to lose you,
and realized I already had
We never even got our goodbye,
and yet I know yours better than the hundreds I've heard
The hugs you continue giving me in my dreams
have become too real to un-feel
I'd still give up everything I've gained to hold your hand;
to have one more hour of those timber-brown eyes,
which I remain convinced must be harboring Eden
It's amazing to me how the seasons
don't quite change without you here
The days just ache like eyes which no longer
have enough power left in them to focus;
the cruelty in that being the ability to go on trying
It wasn't my heart which fell for you;
nor my mind, eyes, soul, or senses
It was me
The same me who'd call when you were home with the flu,
just to make sure you had someone to talk to
The same me who'd save your seat on the bus,
so that you'd be around to make January feel a little less cold
The same me who'll never be satisfied
without your love in my life
Because now that I know everyone's capable of crying
...
I don't want to cry anymore

Battle Cry of the Unjust Sunset

Take up thy sword, and pierce the calm
which these lonely river waters do not deserve
Leave bravery to the tadpoles...

Cut By the Blue

There's a dream I've been having
in which I actually get to hold you;
where this world stays perfect
for all that I'm feeling,
and you fall in love with me

But the skies we now face are so different
I fear I'll never be near you again
And you probably did little more than like me
Guess that's why we call it a dream

I had every intention of being around
Feels like forever
since the last time I sat beside you
So when I say, "This is goodbye."
I only hope you know of the hello(s) to come

Underwater Rainstorms

Among a patch of carved pumpkins;
bright with terrors' shadowy luminescence,
along the banks of a wooded midnight stream,
sits a creature, so beautiful, and yet so alone
that she never cries tears, for there's no one to notice
...
Love letters meant for some anyone flow out of her fingers;
written in water with nowhere to go
For once one has beaten the path to her den
they'll have become too frightened to open their eyes
...
So there she remains; a goddess with no worship,
and her idolatry exists only in men's dreams
Lonely in creek-beds which know
too much sorrow to wrinkle
her cute little fingertips, drowning unspoken words;
beneath that face in the moon which lost its grin long ago
...
Yet hope is still present (perhaps not in her heart, but)
in the desire that drives a man to look upon an owl,
and see those harbored sentiments
she shook free from her hair
when it was perched in her forest; reading an inkless diary
so full of a love which nobody's known
...
Yes, hope is always there
For when the time comes to call back her night-bird,
she may find that his tranquil heart follows

Middle Earth Souls

You ponder pink waterfalls
along the rings of Saturn,
which you were able to view from one of its moons
I consider Egyptian temples,
and spells performed on the streets of Atlantis
You talk of chasing Bigfoot through the hollows,
and giant squid attacking Viking fleets
I dream (like a mastermind) of Elves, and talking whales,
and winds I'd happily control
Maybe we're crazy;
just hopelessly mad
But I couldn't care less
I've got you

Careworn Cloudbursts

I can think about, but not recall
the many hundreds of lines I've lost in my head
I apologize for that misfortune
But it does help me to see that
when dreams are burning in our beings,
we should be burning with them
For they may be ash by morning,
and we will have missed an opportunity
to give the conscious tongue
something new to taste

CHAPTER TWO
-For the April Hagers
of the World-

The Heart Is Always Bleeding

...

Dusk Fire

...

Lazy Candy

...

Glass Eyes

...

Beauty Sleep

...

Pitiful Disease

...

Cry, Little Sister

...

Silenced By Comfort

...

The Disturbing Depth of Perfection

...

Haunts

...

Figmental

...

Lullabubble

The Heart Is Always Bleeding

By now I'm sure she believes
that I've forgotten all about her,
but all I've left behind me
is a future lived without her
The easy part is knowing
that I'll never stop feeling this way,
but she's not here to look in my tears,
and see what I can't say
And though the heart is always bleeding,
the mouth can't always speak
That's what she doesn't understand
That's why she thinks I'm weak
That's also why I have to call her;
let this bleeding heart be heard
Communicate the love I was left with,
even if I can't speak the word
Silent may be the only way
for us to have this conversation
Either way, I need her to know
that she owns my dedication
She's the reason that I feel guilty
when I try getting on with my life
She's the excuse I have for avoiding
any woman who'd make a good wife
My heart is always bleeding;
one love it just hides away,
until the girl crawls back under my skin,
and feels what I'm trying to say

Dusk Fire

I'm in the company of dreamers,
in fields of midnight fireflies
The rains sift this dirty world for a nest to fall clean upon,
as we attempt chanting them away with our strumming

Here I welcome the angel's undertones;
tottering light upon my heart
She soars on vocal blades of shadows;
brightening them, as though they were more
than mere effect

Now whimpers the breeze with a frightful hum
But we, ourselves, haunt; too immersed to fear
After all, what doesn't bleed
thrives to heal the wounds of what does
So we simply dance upon its semblance

Here, all of the beautiful dreamings canker clear the clouds;
lay open our witching hour to Luna, spinning her crown
A giggle, all about her glow
And the angel continues her singing,
and we will continue to play…

until a lion walks the sunrise,
and lays waste to this gathering of gods

Lazy Candy

On my birthday she gave me a shoebox
full of letters she never sent
She just wanted me to know that I stayed on her mind
Years' worth of words she'd forgotten to say
lay housed in a box which
smelled just like childhood,
and gave back so many memories, that you'd swear
(if only for the moment) I was remade
She said she had never read them;
she just wrote them, and hid them
So she wasn't exactly sure
how much she was giving away
But she knew it was better
they were never re-penned,
because the morning doesn't always agree
with what the heart had in mind
And, as I read through them, I was sorry
that all of this time had been wasted;
that it took a box full of hidden hurts
to finally make me feel it
But there's still love for me in that heart of hers,
which I'm slowly rediscovering
At long last, I've blown out these candles
without any wishes born upon that breath,
because it's only little boys who break hearts
that need wish

Glass Eyes

Don't darken another day just because
you can't see yourself as others do
For the spirit wasn't made to reflect;
it can but carry and shine
Thus, if your eyes are shot, perhaps
you were meant to see the world as a blur
No good comes of the ungrateful razor
It will only draw more blood

Whether we work with stuffed animals or elements,
change is what we force upon the world
We may nearly destroy it,
then take satisfaction in its remaining beauty,
but we are unlikely to change our ways alongside sad songs

So hide your face in layers,
and thereby uncover your own shortcomings
You'd return to somewhere,
but you've been nowhere;
choosing dormant seasons full of hibernating time

Tears fall because we hide,
and chance is all that's lost
Walls become a thing of comfort,
because every mirror is faltered

As the dead would tell us;
life will not be withheld
It will age and decease,
and you'll find the notion of material
is immaterial with regard to relevance
The waiting is of no worth

Therefore savor what speaks to the soul;
That you can suffer, but never save
For this all we will have worth having
when the lonely nights become realities

Open your mind to your heart,
and the hearts of others;
even if your vision isn't as clear as glass
Choose a life a peaceful commemoration;
one which requires only that you smile until you cry,
and cherish any love found along the road there and back
Then you can simply keep doing this
until all of your days are done

Beauty Sleep

I remember when you brought
all of that yarn to school
Yards of braided string
you were so adorably proud of;
openly airing the secrets
of that magical little mind you dwell within,
and a class of cold children just couldn't understand
I wish someone would reassure me
that I'm not the only one who finally does

I remember the day I realized
what the word love is meant to mean
You were alone on a stage, singing that song
which still makes you blush every time I bring it up
I turned to Thomas, and told him that I loved you
And, though I'd never actually thought about it
before that very moment, I knew this was something
which could never be taken back
But I laughed it off to keep from crying,
and continued listening to you breaking my heart

I remember every little moment with you
that I've been blest enough to have
You never lost those things which made you undeniable
And I fail to see how I could love you better,
just knowing that no one will ever love you more
than this friend whom you will always have

Pitiful Disease

She's betraying herself
to make him happy,
and I can't stop blaming a memory
It's tragic that her masks
are now all she has,
but she's violently torn
between woman and girl;
missed seeing her self
through all of that makeup
So she's lost her dreams to his altar,
and I can't stop blaming the memory

Cry, Little Sister

It's hard to imagine tears in those eyes,
but that's exactly what I picture
when I think of a heart breaking
For a break is what would become of my heart
if I ever actually did see you cry
That would paralyze every nerve in me
which it possibly could,
then leave me here to hear nothing;
save my broken heart beating

Silenced By Comfort

I never want the world to know
the beautiful words you gave to me
to hold onto,
to drown beneath,
to live and die by
I don't want another ear to hear any of those things,
so that I can still think of myself
as the luckiest man alive;
then die knowing I was blest
by sentences nobody else will ever hear again

The Disturbing Depth of Perfection

She autographs the world around her
with lip-gloss and a smile
She buries the harshness of all my worries
with touchable words and blind fingers
Her breath's not as warm as her heart,
but what it lacks in heat it overcomes with sentiment
And, though we'll always own each other
in wildly different ways,
slaves of love don't dance upon level ground

Haunts

There are things we see and feel
which we don't explain, yet don't deny
A mother lies awake at night,
and listens to her dead child cry
Things which chill us, through and through
Things which stab us, me and you
Mental nightmares we'll run into;
that which we believe that can't be true
Or can it?

We dream in adoring darkness;
the same darkness we come to fear,
as we hide beneath our blankets
from nothing seen, year after year
An unforgiving figure stares at you
through a window, as he glows in the night
Darker than your imagination's ever been,
but it's gone when you attempt second sight
Was it real?

A late phone call from no one's received
Something whispers when you're alone
The shadows seem to move around you
Your door creeps open on its own
How do you forget what shouldn't happen?
How do you tell a lie to your mind?
Your eyes are open, and won't close
Your thoughts linger in a fearsome bind,
but over what?

Ghosts hide within our perception,
and death cackles within our heads
But if visions are morbid delusions,
we're most prone to them in our beds

We see more than what's there to be seen
We hear more than what's there to be heard
We feel more than what's there to be felt,
because haunts speak louder than words

Figmental

There is a space in each thought
where my dreams come alive,
where my hopes are immortalized;
there my essence derives
Here all mythology spurs,
and all fantasies confide
There all hatred falls,
and all the cosmos collide

There is talk here with syllables which do not exist;
a budding telepath's annunciation
We are warm here beneath a snow-riddled canopy;
courting figmental mutations

Riding dragons among the landscape,
where acrylic acres paint themselves
Sentiment cannot depict how it feels
to see Unicorns stride alongside Elves
Mystics marry wizards with rings of lightning;
love and magic makers in four dimensions
Evil picnics upon the harvest hillsides,
having lost all malicious intentions

More than one heart can contain,
this peaceful decimation
And my eyes desire closure,
seeing figmental permeation

Taste the dead improbable
with each breath that you survive
Trust your feet when on the minefield
Know that alone is still alive
Greater than grandeur, and more false than lies
As raw as existence, and feeding blue skies
...

Lullabubble

Teddy bears protect the small room where she sleeps
The moon on her mountain almost covers the sky
Her palms are always concealed in her sleeves
And I'd be blissful, forever, just watching her breathe

All I want in a woman is tangled up in her hair
I'm convinced that her laughter created the breeze
Safe in a soft heart, whose fires are always kind
She's the never-ending slumber growing my dreams

How did this angel come to be with me?
How can I be sure that she can do more than bless?
Does she love me?
Can she love me?
Am I the dreamer giving her wings?

She can't watch 'The Lion King' without crying,
and says she's always crying harder on the inside
Still as warm as the child I knew, now gone
Her eyes dance around the magic
so evident in those tears

Sweetness lingers upon all she touches
Her smile will haunt every beating heart
Even her sadnesses glimmer
And I'd be blissful, forever, just watching her breathe

CHAPTER THREE

-Rock -N- Ramble-

Hoodrats and Hangovers

...

Why Loving You Is Painful / Why Hating You
Is Wrong

...

The End of Always and Forever

...

Bubbles in Boxes

...

Unloved and Unknown

...

Just to Smile Again

...

What I Know to Be True

...

Doves with Dirty Wings

...

You

...

Concrete Flowers

...

Night Eyes

...

Childhood's End

Hoodrats and Hangovers

We survived sixteen
by driving our hangovers away
Those ten perfect minutes of the morning
always got us home
And, though these memories are full of holes,
they still manage to keep me warm

The year was a gorgeous stream of heartbreak,
but our bonds wouldn't drown
The roads remained our getaway,
even if we didn't get very far
I admit, I've lost some friends as of late,
but only the ones that I needed to lose

It's been such a long time
since I could honestly claim a best friend;
even good ones have seemed so hard to come by
But I'm through with that truth
I refuse to miss it,
and, with a little luck, I'll never have to miss you
...
We survived sixteen
by letting large parts of us perish
Somewhere between the alcohol and tears,
we did a lot of dying,
but I'm glad to have lived through it;
so thankful to still have you with me..

no longer gripping a bottle,
and learning how to survive without it

Why Loving You Is Painful / Why Hating You Is Wrong

I am yours...
The dragon's tear;
lonely and frozen where I should feel at home
The glimmer slave;
dazzled and broken wherever I should fall

You're a blinding contradiction of
hard darkness and intense light;
arresting to
my shattered emotions
It's true,
and I love only you

You are mine...
The splintered glass;
puzzle of a mirror, so hard on the hands
Like ceramic silk;
flowing, yet rough, and toy of the masochist

Like a Valentine;
the idea is well-meaning, but the doubt which follows giving
hears a thesaurus recited in planned apology
And we can't betray potential;
just fail to realize what it might have meant
for us

Your dragon's tear;
hardened before I hit the ground
Your glimmer slave;
in poor pieces to make you happy

The End of Always and Forever

I'm payback in a corner
I'm revenge in a frown
I'm liquor and broken glass,
drinking myself down

I'm pain in the darkness
I'm blood in your piss
I'm a cold electric current
within a passionate kiss

I'm the irony in each dream
I'm a thirst inside your bones
I'm the edge which scathes your skin
when you get beat with stones

I'm a razor in your eye
I'm dread upon your face
I'm like one hot coal
upon a cool bed of lace

I'm all that you believe in
I'm also what you fear
I'm the result of every attempt;
that tear, now here, my dear

Bubbles in Boxes

My spirit left my core last night
It fled my body, passed through a window,
and shot down the road;
speed ever gaining in its unencumbered light,
as if time were some dying root
of a seed it had long-since sewn
Then it was slowed by your walls, hung up in your room;
where it stayed,
watching you dream beneath your skin
Long dreams of peace and love and gloom,
from which
all of your auburn days begin
It stroked your face
like a knowing breeze
which would never be allowed to grow old,
and kissed your mouth with such ease
that your fingers were opened;
warm in place of cold
It left you waking with a smile;
one which greeted
all of the sun's light
This frosted softness into your style,
and turned all of your
destructive wrongs right
Today you kissed the side of my grin,
and rubbed your nose against mine
as you said,
"I'm not sure that I know where to begin...
You were in my dreams,
and I can't get you out of my head."
Then after a moment of taking it in,
I replied by saying
"I belong in that bed."

You snorted, but quickly stopped,
and whispered softly,
"I think I love you."
I chuckled, and murmured back,
"That must've been one hell of a dream."
Then we both laughed,
until the moment trailed far behind us;
leaving us in a coil of gentle glances
None too soon you said,
"I feel like I'm already in your arms."
And so, we stood still,
not really knowing what to do;
just letting the world spin around us...

Unloved and Unknown

I often speak least
when I've got the most to say
about those important things;
us, love, and (as always) what's gone wrong
We're forever filling these empty spaces
with words which get us nowhere
I often wish I could have friends
who care about me
as much as I care about them...
Why am I the one who's always calling?
Sometimes I feel more than a little trapped
within my own condition
I love and hate myself in almost equal amounts
It's tough to help me smile,
but generally harder to empty me of hope
I'm often able to see just how alone I actually am
Today I cried, and there was nobody to notice
Who was here to stop the pain?
No one
I often understand
that I'm worth more than I let myself see
And, so long as I hold my heart back,
my alias could forever be
'he who none know to love'

Just to Smile Again

A lot of shit happens, and a lot of paths change
We may find ourselves far from where we begin
We've fallen apart; I can't kill this pain,
and I would give my life just to smile again

Yes, my lady, my blessing, my soul;
never hearing that voice has taken its toll
It's not enough just admitting I miss you
Without you here, I won't get through

You used to say, "Smile for me."
Now all I can do is cry
I pushed you away so long ago
that I no longer remember why
Your memory invades my dreams,
like shadows I can't overtake
So, now I'm trying to avoid the pain
by keeping myself awake
You're still so fucking close,
so why does it seem so far?
I wish there were a way for me
to make it to where you are

If we could just get together, and talk,
then you'd see that I still care;
that I love you more than most would try,
and I only want to be there

A lot of shit happens, and a lot of friends leave
We go so far from where we begin
And I hope these words help you to believe
what it would mean just to see you again

Yes, my homie, my brother, my true;
nothing is quite the same without you
We miss you, still, and everything hurts
without you here to dust off the dirt
You were leaving the day I returned;
nowhere to be found when I needed my friend
And I'm not trying to point fingers,
but life broke what I thought couldn't bend
You let me see what I wanted from others
You were the pal which no one's outdone

Someone who helped me to love myself better?
You've been the only one
You continue to lift me up,
even now that you're not around
I know how hard her love hit you
Wish I could change the way it went down

So bring yourself back here where you belong,
and you'll realize how much you are needed
I know we'd all do what we are able
to make sure the past isn't repeated

A lot of shit happens, and too many people die
Without your guidance, where do I begin?
Wishing and praying now, as I cry;
knowing I'd trade our places to see your smile again

Yes, my keeper, my break, and my bend;
just know that I'll love you well beyond the end
Reminiscent of years you lived to see;
I'm standing because you'd want me to be

I treasure those little things we did;
a hundred days spent in the park
I remember going swimming, then picking berries
All around my room lives your mark
You had a kindness which was all your own,
and you cared more than I could care for me
You had talents which breathe to this day,
but to the living you're much a mystery
Your death brought tears to my father's eyes;
the first time he'd cried since grandpa passed
And I know you'll be the one waiting
to comfort me as I breathe my last

If I need you, I'll look into my heart
You'll guide me within my dreams
You left behind a legacy of love,
so this isn't as bad as it seems

A lot of shit happens, and a lot can go wrong
No, we will not stop where we begin
But our days won't always be so hopelessly long
We will find some way to smile again

What I Know to Be True

The world looks colder without a bed to sleep in,
and my eyes look older as the darkness deepens
But I've always preferred a cloudy sky,
and truth's just reality if you don't value the lie
So it need come as no surprise to see me
close and cry

Doves with Dirty Wings

The first tear drops as the last sun sets
Her love for him, she won't forget
The empty bottle's broken against each wall,
as she's screamed and bled and taken his fall
She's forgiven these beatings over and over,
hoping that one night he'd come home sober
But life tests its lessons, and he's never passed
She was in the fast lane until he drove her to last
...
So, where should a battered lover go from here?
Home's been this puddle of bloody beer
Is there more than a nightmare
when waking from fear?
Weakness won't help you survive

You

Your love keeps me going
Your smile lights the way
Your voice brings the sun
which brightens my day
Your touch gives me hope
Your soft words are sweet
Your eyes hold the shine
that's guiding my fleet
Your straight, raven hair
gets tangled by the air
It compliments that pretty face
All I can do is stare
You know this feeling won't fade
Our hearts do but beckon the flame
And, though we commit the crimes,
our love takes the blame

Concrete Flowers

From us pouring out our drinks to show respect for the dead,
to talking like old poets; birthing gold in our heads
Dying our greaser hair, then fighting on trampolines
Sitting out on sidewalks and making fun of fiends
Strolling down dark roads, and looking up at the stars
Playing Hide-And-Go-Seek, and trying to play guitars

Close enough to cry in front of you,
and not worry about my pride
We've got each other; that's all that matters,
so there's nothing here to hide
The best person I could hope to find
when I know that I need a friend
We will always have that brotherly love,
so please don't try to pretend
about your tears,
about your fears,
and never about who you are

Rapping on the playground; war games, and King of the Hill
I was down with you then, so know I'm down with you, still
Experts of the scare, miniature golf, tricks of the trade,
deep conversations, intuitive notions, and sharing shade
Playing Monopoly until dawn
We never finished that five-dollar game
The world may change around us, but our bond is forever the same
Drinking champagne, and laying out in the snow
Ouija boards, campsites; things I haven't let go

So just know that you need not pretend
about your tears,
about your fears,
and never about who you are

Night Eyes

You were beautiful to me when your eyes met the moon,
but that wasn't enough to make January into June
You took such comfort in love, like you were tenderly hypnotized
And I loved you in love, my love, but when falling we improvise

Sometimes your voice is there to greet the dawn,
but waking I realize the fantasy it was;
meant to remind me of us
Whenever the comets are out I feel your fingers in my hair,
but the winds die, and I must focus

Falling in love shattered me
It left me breathless, but alive
And now, so deathly cold to the world, I've no good reason to survive
Genuine is my memory of you lashing out at the stars
Original is my denial and hatred toward these scars

Sometimes your shadow touches me in the dark,
but when the light appears,
no one is there; I stand alone
Streetlights in trees may capture the scent of your smile,
but the sun destroys what little lavender I could call my own

The moonlit night can bring you back,
but the sun eviscerates my love
So you live and die from night to day,
and we're never together long enough
I merely miss an experience;
one person who changed my simple all
You've begun to clothe your tears,
but I'm not convinced you survived that fall
No ma'am, I still can't hate you
Those lies I will never despise
What I can't manage is forgiving myself
for ever losing your eyes;
baby blue, lovely you

I would look to tomorrow, but I can't recall much of anything
with you gone, and myself to remind
I would move on, but I keep right on believing you're still here,
when it's clear that you've left me behind

...my love

Childhood's End

Open my heart, and find that it's empty
Desire was there, but priorities change
A blood-filled cavity
is all that's left to be had
And, though my eyes haven't aged,
I am older;
a little colder, and missing myself
Nothing's new this time around
It all lacks the feeling
which first made it move
My mind is frozen;
broken by the dust of repetition,
whose form is wrinkling and slow
This I'm to yearn for?
Only death undying
and hollow hearts crying
fill the life beyond childhood's end

CHAPTER FOUR
-The Sundown (Gone Grey)-

Wither-Bloom

...

Electric Ice

...

All There Is to Say

...

A Talent for Lacking

...

Evol

...

Living by Mandatory Order

...

Chasing the Day Before the Dawn

...

Maybe This Is Right

...

Soulstain

...

Shadows in Ice

...

Bent Swirls and Hoodwinked Luster

...

Mile 81

Wither-Bloom

Down calls the mountain
the soft fogs of former rains;
hiding river gray

Drowned in a fountain,
let free, flow a thousand pains;
softly bleeding May

Born amongst the ghosts
which blow the winds through willows,
sheltered miles of rust

Crowned, the snow cloud boasts
of all the treasures he throws
down to winters lust

Out eased the blue bird,
nesting so safe in the shade,
to soar like a god

Though their words aren't heard,
the blooms shout out as they fade;
mocking voice for fraud

Last to fall for fear
that it might not touch the ground,
that single leaf sways

Broken on their ears,
waves sigh for themselves the sound
haunting darkest days

Electric Ice

It's hard to say whom the rain falls for
Is it for me, or for you, or perhaps for other shattered dreamers?
Gray days and dead winds
Dispositions which staple themselves in my eyes
And I won't talk about the love I'm not feeling,
because that love truly hates what I've become
So, beyond this emptiness, I've nothing to offer
Life beats my skull against its concrete
until I'm a good deal more than bloodshot
This cold afternoon of umbrellas and tears
makes me consider that there may be a shade darker than black;
a nameless presence which navigates
the murky waters of the spirit,
and gives those depths more reason to be dreaded
Still, I'm more fearful of the falling rain,
for it suggests the inevitability of what I'm running from;
sunny time in a world of friendly faces,
where others shall know that my visage truly is
tattered by a gray it could not escape
I see the concussions oncoming,
and fear warmth may place my body in shock
I'm not alive,
I'm simply here;
trapped in a colorblind purgatory of icy ideals
which think in tongues
So, bring me a deep fog;
lose me within it,
and let it end here,
because the rain falls for those with days to look forward to
The clouds hide the sun for me

All There Is to Say

How does knowing
that someone loves you
not move you at all?
How does it feel
to disregard another's heart?
Now, I never claimed to be
some god's gift to women,
I just tried to care for you
And every time I see the way
you draw hearts around my name,
I break wide open from this contrast
of apprehension and misunderstanding
I only ever asked that you never mislead me
And, though it's pretty clear that you care,
I can't place my trust in what you won't
allow yourself to be;
mine
So happiness goes on hiding,
and this is simply where we are...

A Talent for Lacking

A heart that falls
into a love it doesn't believe in
may die with words, but live forever,
and see only another's reflection
in the mirror;
preparing to find
what it's aware was destroyed
But I suppose it's okay to be ready,
even when we lose hope;
for we keep breathing
And, as long as that
keeps our hearts beating,
there is love waiting for us
somewhere in the world

Evol

I long to taste the blood on her lips,
brought forth when the fangs in my eyes
have ripped her open, and finally taken her life
Therefore, what is this love
but her guiltless suicide,
and a new season of drugs for my mortal tongue?

Living by Mandatory Order

Tearing at the flesh beneath my skin;
the worms have come out to play
This is the world I'm made to live in
This is the reason we're dying today
Before the fight, the battle's lost,
so rip the fears from my brain;
the sickness from my blood,
name your cost,
or tomorrow we rise up slain
Freeze each perversion until they've fled
Hold my hand, and show me love
Take these acute thoughts
out of my head,
until your nearness is enough
Stop plaguing me with customary ways
Teach me to like the colors in my soul
Let me quicken, don't toss me delay,
for societies worms are taking their toll

Chasing the Day Before the Dawn

I've been the one drying her tears,
and holding her world together
when that lucky fool knocks it down

And even though we know
that few could love her better than me,
she's still running afraid

But I dust my heart off,
and put it back in her hands;
hoping someday she'll understand
that what I feel isn't going to fade
...
I've got every reason
to shut her out of my mind;
like the way she doesn't respond
when I ask her to love me
But I still believe she can

If not her than no one
(or so the romantic inside of me screams)

And, though I'm not the dream she wakes to,
though I'm not her autumn breeze,
I need her more than I'm sure I know how to
And, lord knows, one day she'll consider me

Maybe This Is Right

I heard you were asking about me,
and think I may have seen you yesterday
So you know, I'm just existing;
dreaming of our next introduction
At the moment, I like the way we are;
apart
But I'll call you when I'm ready;
when I'm comfortable with myself
Knowing me, that may never happen,
and not seeing you every day has me
regretting the choices I've made
I never meant to hurt you,
or make you feel alone
I'd run, but I'm afraid I'd hurt you more
Do you even care anymore?
Maybe I'm not supposed to know
At the least, I know I'm on your mind
And, for now, that's enough

Soulstain

Sometimes I feel like I've drowned
in the beauty around me,
but inside I stay alive
I should have called more often
I should have slain this trepidation
I should have been there for you,
but I let my ego prevent the rest of me from loving
Life goes on, as it would have
had we never met
I live each day fighting our death,
but when I'm sleeping
your words come alive
And, as I cry freely there in your arms,
my hearts takes (what it wishes were)
its final breath...
But soon the sun is in my ears again;
forcing me out of bed,
making me carry on,
when all I want to do is fall into your eyes

Shadows in Ice

Bury this soul in the sea
to ensure that it's forever haunted, not haunting
And, when it snows in Eden,
surely the goddess will pray
on frozen knees with stone-struck seraphs...
...that our hearts might beat again
...that our minds may breathe again
...that the seasons continue in change
to ensure that we remain

Bent Swirls and Hoodwinked Luster

Only half a moon left shining on me;
makes me wonder if my fingernails
could really indicate I'm cared for
Asking myself how many people are forgetting me,
as the white slowly fades from my cuticles
Trying harder now to convince myself
that I believe I'm loved,
since there's no way I can ever actually be sure
And this rings true for everyone

But everything I've ever wanted to be, I'm becoming
And maybe these eyes are but choosing
to see a waning crescent in the sky
According to my calendar,
the damn thing is waxing back to its full glory
But anyone who thinks of it as round
knows it's never truly full;
that's only how we perceive it to be

I think perspective is what I'm hinting at here
That word which gets us everywhere,
and never really goes anywhere

At times I think I'm immature
for putting so much energy into that orb,
but it won't share my secrets with anyone
It will never not be up there
And, as the evening darkens,
it seems to be all I can see

Mile 81

Back and forth
across the skyline at dawn,
I begin to resent all the things I've loved
But the ambient cloud cover dries my emotion
before it turns to tears,
and takes my control;
along with any thoughts leading me back to you

But watching the pink turn gray
is like watching myself become cold,
and watching the treetops change
is like watching my love get old

I'm lost again in Mile 81;
seeing only my state, not the state I'm in
Lost for good in Mile 81;
wishing to be back with you again

Brittle bones break beneath my bitter heartbeat,
but I can't bother with that just now
For the road has gotten as quick as your affection ever was,
and this land is but a pool of bloody honey
I'm afraid I'll never outrun

So, watching the suns disarray
is like watching myself go blind
Watching each sign fade the day,
with nothing left ahead or behind

And still I'm lost in Mile 81;
knowing no pain as I let go of the wheel
Destined to cease in Mile 81;
I close my eyes, and refuse to heal

Forever lost in Mile 81
I only want to be with you again
Never to leave Mile 81
Wishing you could be here for the end...

CHAPTER FIVE
-Consecrating Flame-

The Way I'm Really Feeling

...

Seasonal

...

Burnouts and Blowpops

...

Left-Handed Hearts

...

The Ecstasy of Ice: Keeper's Final Entry

...

It's Never November Without You

...

The Price of Blood

...

Thespian

...

Soft Skin, Frail Value

...

Unspoken

...

Quibbles of the Angel's Allure

...

Let the Demon Dream

The Way I'm Really Feeling

It's confusing...
but I'm glad that much is understood
And it's nothing I can't handle;
at least, I hope it's not
For her breath is laden with warmth,
as she spews soft and heartfelt words
that blend all too well in my ears
I can only take so much
Like any man who's ever lived,
I'm afraid of loving too much of her,
then never being able to let go
....
And so, oblivious
to the obviousness of my love,
I continue drowning;
never dying, simply sinking
But don't think I'm breaking down
...
This is nothing I can't handle

53

Seasonal

Success is budding, blossom like;
preparing to live again
Rushing to an awakening;
inspiring the year to begin
Numbness turns its callous to warmth, and
gust-full green ascends

Surging beams of blissful heat are
underscored where derived
Memories bathe in bashful waters;
moments which tans revive
Ecstatic stars compliment new nights
Rustically, we survive

From the earthy core of a dying beauty,
autumn conceives its browning heart
Lovers dream a waking breeze, which
lasting change will war apart

Whispering fire and cold fluff
infiltrate stone-covered foes
Never deadening daylight winds
twirl the merry-land snows
Each flake-filled cloud within the sky is
raging, at odds with our toes

And time is ever scented with seasons

Burnouts and Blowpops

I saw your picture in the paper;
taken at a local football game,
looking as happy as you stay in my memories
And photos which capture us that accurately are a rarity
Somehow, seeing it made everything okay

I'd be lying if I said I've missed you
Truth is, I'd overlooked us until now
But it's nice to know that you can still smile;
given this dying magic which is changing us forever,
and the colder versions of ourselves being found in these same old spaces

How could I ever forget?
You smoked your Blacks, and drank your beers
long before the school bells would ring
Carrying a purse when you needed a backpack,
and laughing about how you lost your virginity
to a wannabe thug who couldn't got the job done
Armando asleep in the floor between our desks;
head on your thigh, and a hand on your ass

You were always getting me into trouble;
sensing how important it is that the world think
I'm a lot less serious than I truly am

Now I find myself wishing that someone would wake me from this dream
which I've been through more times than could ever be necessary,
because the people I used to know
around this town I used to love
are still there;
they're still beautiful
And I'm so much better than I was before

So let us go there again, however we're able
For I only have winter to look forward to
And, though I've been living without you
(though you'd never know it to look at me),
I still need the friends I let scatter
And, love withstanding, they still need me

Left-Handed Hearts

I would give all that I am now
to have back what I was
Tear away the day like red rose petals,
and bleed in the settling dust;
just to find you in time

A butterfly shatters my window
on a frosty summer day,
melts into a pile of snow,
and burns itself away;
leaving me with broken glass

I would betray all aspects of my mind
if I could but love again
Despise my only gray soul
to make now enough,
and reopen your hands

A breeze shatters my wisdom,
and discovers my soft spot,
evaporates into clouds of hail,
and makes the day hot;
leaving me broken

Now I'm crying blood;
shifting upon the glass
with this emptiness at home in my eyes,
and only a shadow left to call a soul
I'm cold in a memory
with my left-handed heart

The Ecstasy of Ice: Keeper's Final Entry

I thought I could become too cold to cry,
but I was wrong...
For, without my hope,
all I have are tears

And, dreamland help me, I'm unsure

I thought I could live without the old world
Who knew it would keep on
spinning without me?

And do I have the nerve to join it again?

Now I must open every door I have closed,
and I've thrown all the keys away

But there is sun in the windows
I'm not afraid to climb

This ice can't last forever,
but what's still warm beneath it can

The season's changed, and so have I
So, melt these frowns, and let me grow again

It's Never November Without You

The nights continue to get colder,
and I hate it now more than ever
Having to admit
that I don't know who you've become
has taken more time than I thought I'd be given
But, here I am... still
And I haven't forgotten you
like my mother once assured me I would
I'm no longer insecure,
but I'm a far cry from confident
...
I so want to believe
that all of those pictures I drew for you
are still covering your walls,
or that you long to have them there again
if they're not
For you're the girl I think of
when I hear a pretty word;
all of those cute, little terms
I was always too shy to give you
And there's enough distance between us now
to hide everything we once had
All I want you to know,
though I'm sure people are tired
of hearing me say it,
is that I miss waking up to a world with you in it
I should be glowing this late in the year,
but it's never November without you

The Price of Blood

We've talked to death about life,
and falsified proof of the nothing

I've got a story to tell,
I've got people to miss,
and, above all, memories to cherish

We treated railways like sidewalks;
never wished to walk on water
We had enough to busy our lives
without the stress of saving the world
We piled the loose stakes for reasons unknown,
and contemplated who we were to become
We had the dreams,
and we had the heart,
but it's plain to see that we took those for granted;
failing to notice how high the stakes
were stacking against us
Now, I still feel your sorrow;
those sad eyes with nowhere to turn
Trying to piece things together, we lost our dreams,
and that once-precious sensitivity became dark;
as red as an open wound
But at night I still dream about kids;
the kids we were,
and the vision we shared
When it's quiet I hear the happy times,
and for the moment I am happy once more...

Thespian

Locked on a stage with the familiar unknown
Bedazzling strange faces with your talents;
with abilities which overthrow
all these emotional monsters have learned
Making the seams of others' heart bleed out
in such sweet desperation

Cry we will if that's your way
Cry we shall if that's your will

You're the space extolled between each line;
manufactured perfection among
the written syllables which we would not
dare to breathe
You are *the* chosen emotion;
Able to exhale your humanity,
and have it heard without the words
which most must say

Cry we will if that's your way
Cry we shall if that's your will

Soft Skin, Frail Value

I knew I'd regret it, but I went ahead and did it
I took the first thing she offered,
with no regard for her heart;
like every man who came before me
But I'm not walking away,
because I really do care for her
in spite of my actions

...

She was always better to me
than anyone had to be
She's tried so hard to love too many;
doing only what they ask for,
and ending up worse than alone
So, where others run from her,
I'm running to her,
and being whatever she needs

...

She probably went home, and cried
She probably had no one to call
She probably spent the night in the shower,
convinced that she'd lost another friend
But I'm calling first thing in the morning
to thank her for all the ways she's supported me,
for her rights are not to blame for my wrongs
And, as for that part of her heart which I've taken,
I'll be giving back until she has
a greater portion of my own

Unspoken

I was dreaming of you when the phone woke me up
I'm always a little scared that someone's calling to tell me you're gone
By all logical assumptions, you should be;
should have been a long time ago

But it was only you on the line
Surprisingly sober this morning, and reminding me
that I'm depriving you of what you believe you need;
me by your side

Presumably so that you can feel like you're some part of my life;
trying to be a piece of the man who once could've given the whole
Scattering sentiments laced with the persuasions of sorrow

But you'll never love me as you do your alcohol,
and to your mind I'm merely a detail that's keeping you
from finding a sense of completion we both know you'll never feel

You're right about a lot of things
I will regret this decision of distance when you do finally pass away,
but not for the reasons you believe

I was a child without a father;
that, I can forgive but never condone
Because I'm no longer that child,
and all I know about you is summed up by the way you smell
I'm seventeen years old, and that's still all I really know
It's not my fault, though I once thought it was

Hell, I'm almost a man now,
and I don't even want you as a friend
For a father is someone who knows and loves his son,
and you only love the idea that you have one

Quibbles of the Angel's Allure

People think she's a smoker because she always carries a lighter
Some kind of superstition, I'm guessing,
for I've never seen her do more than light a candle with it
And those little lights were made to make mouths water,
for they give her a nonsensical excuse to make brownies
in the middle of whatever it was she was doing
This way there's still a little more time left
before she has to be alone again

Of course, if I had it my way, she never would be alone,
but I'm only a lonely pretty boy
(or a man, it's all the same)
who has to be lured into saying what he's feeling;
though I'm sure she already sees it
I mean, how could she not?
...Anyway,
there's usually a scratch-n-sniff sticker stuck to her;
just wherever she happens to put it,
and begging someone to get closer

Her childish sensuality is heartwarming,
with the power to overcome my inhibitions
And, before I understand what it is I should be feeling
(whether ice cold or nervous to a breaking point),
I'm swiftly filled with such a smug type of glow
that immaculate solace flows from my mind
to spill through my mouth;
making me wish I had a pen
And her eyes darken to a dazzle...
Her laugh is the sweetest little delight
It's got a way of raining all around me
And whenever I want to drown out the world,
I simply let it come and cover me

I don't know who I am to her,
only what I want her to be to me
And maybe I'm luckier than I believe
(I'd like to believe that I am)
For my adoration is dusty, but fully prepared,
to find its next tomorrow by way of her

Let the Demon Dream

In his cage,
the inmate hardens, like the stone walls he has to live with
But the debt is far from paid,
for he demolished his daughter's childhood;
making her play with things other than toys
Thank goodness she was too young to understand
Now that she does,
she's grown out of his sickness,
but her heart is still broken
She will never forget what it was to cry,
to plead, in the arms of a molester
whose lusts only grew with each tear

And, though he will be freed
(likely sooner than later;
let loose like a rabid dog into a naive neighborhood,
with the same sick intentions and urges he's always retained),
I will not be dissuaded from speaking my mind

So, to the one who might give him his rights and realities back,
I beg only that you think of the woman
still as scared as that child she had the misfortune of being;
afraid he'll come back to do more than haunt her
The adult who cries most every night;
terrified of what she'll recall in her sleep
If you were asking me how to deal with this monster
who's almost convinced you he's human,
if you asked how I'd handle the power
of opening the night to his will,
I'd say throw away the key,
and let the demon dream

CHAPTER SIX
-A Winter with No Crows-

The Sadness of the Beautiful

...

Love Is a Battlefield I'm Bleeding Upon

...

Wandering Souls

...

Laughing On the Verge of Tears

...

Thoughts

...

Shiver-Shock Meadow

...

Riddle of the Wind

...

To Help You Understand What I Don't

...

A Fallacy of Myth

...

Hope for Your Heart

...

The Girl Is a Ghost

...

Jack-O-Lantern

The Sadness of the Beautiful

Damn you vulgar stars
what sit in the black seas,
and remain oblivious
as to why you are burning
Your hearts are ablaze with passion,
but you are not in need of another;
therefore you torch any lover
who dares to hold you
And the million thunderous questions you ask
are answered only by your lonesome,
for you have only yourself
Your flames are the catalyst of every beauty
which you are unwilling to behold
Tis no wonder why your death
is seen as a marvelous thing;
for it's only in death that one hears
all of the fairy tales kept hidden in your core
You're white to the eyes of a blackbird's mind,
and you will die
remembering only the loneliness
of your lifetime;
how cold your fire was,
even when you dreamed

Love Is a Battlefield I'm Bleeding Upon

Go ahead and question my sympathies
Warp these emotions around in that paranoid mouth of yours,
and refuse to really hear me
All of my words are distorted by the time they reach your center;
and that's assuming they manage to get there at all
Even if I thought this war could be won,
I would fall to a loss,
for my enemy's insane
And, rather than believe she's defeated,
the queen would simply deny every drop of blood which was bled
in an effort to keep me out of her heart
...
So, winning her may as well equate to walking away
I know of no way to warm what only grows colder,
and the woman I'm intent upon claiming no longer exists
Therefore, let memory be my bride;
distance, her only imperfection
...
Under the grays, above the reds,
I drop my steel, and kneel
in the damaged presence of her majesty
As a last act of weakness guided by bravery,
I lower my head, and prepare to die
But she kisses me, wounds me, and tells me to live
Then skips away singing like the lass I once knew her to be
I bleed, but I love,
so I breathe just to be
guided out of this fog under the watch of her songs;
as this war converts back to child's play
Her harsh blanket of affection transforms
into something befitting a picnic for the princess and I;
a feast of kindnesses, unbound and unnumbered
And may the loathsome scars help us to stay this way
at least as long as forever

Wandering Souls

I slowly fall asleep,
thinking of the people who are currently my destiny,
and my mind slowly unwinds
Suddenly I'm in a place that's strangely familiar,
but to which I am a stranger
I walk to a nearby hill,
sit in a nearby tree,
and watch the last fallen leaves float gently to the ground
The skies are hopelessly gray,
and I can see for miles
Not a soul in sight, but they're out there;
I can hear their voices caught in the breeze,
and their sadness is so intense that I cry
Lightning strikes randomly,
and when it dies, the wind whispers,
"Another one dead."
Like I said,
here I'm all too aware of every gale-driven prayer and desperate plea
I can feel the pain so deeply that I begin to think I'm bleeding internally
Then yet another cries out...
A young girl steps on a landmine
She was utterly innocent, but it still kills her;
just like that
Another baby is born to starve and die
Life lost before it could really begin;
just like that
A blood transfusion equates to HIV
An unwilling mother will succumb;
just like that
One wrong turn in broad daylight finds a bullet to the head
Another man down;
just like that
The gusts suddenly stop,
and I awake with the sun; only to find that I'm still crying
It's a bit strange;
I went to bed contemplating how bad I have it,
and now that notion's been destroyed
For I've realized that in that dream
I was simply seeing the world as it is

We plague each other mercilessly
We destroy ourselves
And, to most, innocence is only a word
Love is something lost in the blink of an eye,
because we throw it in the air without wings to fly
And so, to that soul wandering on the breeze,
may you continue to carry
until the lightning finally passes us by;
assuming it ever passes us by

Laughing On the Verge of Tears

She took off her mask, not to mention her shoes,
and laughed coolly on the verge of tears;
as she began to realize how much I really remembered,
and to see how kiddish I remained
I suppose she was expecting to find a cold-hearted man,
which I am to a certain degree,
but she doesn't deserve to see that
while I've still got a better side to show her

She hopped onto my bed, and danced to the song in the air;
steadily changing the lyrics to matters relating to us
I almost couldn't believe that she still felt so at home with me
after all of the time which had gone by,
but we've always walked that obscured road
between friends and lovers
Let us never question the welcome rarity of finding someone
who's actually willing to stand beside us, unaccompanied,
in a world playing 'follow the leader'

She left through the window, because it was there,
and she wanted me to see *her* every time I saw *it*
Getting in her car, she looked back to say,
"If we happen to lose each other again,
like we always manage to do, just reclaim this moment,
and never doubt that we'll find our way back...
I know this is where I'm supposed to tell you I love you,
but I won't. Hell, if you don't see that by now,
then you'll always be lost... but that kind of works for me."

She slowly pulled away with all of the windows down,
singing some silly song we'd made up years ago
And I sat there in the window,
already wanting to see her again...
laughing on the verge of tears

Thoughts

Sometimes I think that nightmares
exist to balance things out
when they get too good
Sometimes I think that worry
is the most pointless of distractions
We've all got problems
No cause for concern
Sometimes I think that I'll be forgotten
if I attempt to love myself better
Others want comfort for themselves,
not to know you're at your best

...

Sometimes I wish the sun
would miscarry its rise
When darkness is all that I long to know,
it feels nice to dive where light doesn't live
Sometimes I wish that love were mandatory;
forcing beauty upon the animosity,
like some daydreamer's utopia
Sometimes I wish that I could understand
how other people hope to see me,
so I'd know what it is they've been seeing
but not saying;
as much of what we think goes unknown
in more than one mind

...

Shiver-Shock Meadow

I move quickly between these willows
I tread fast upon this snow
Her flawless eyes gleam among the shadows
I can't hold her, nor let go
A weave of warmth in each stare she throws
I die to flavor, seeing her mouth close
The skies turn gray, this blizzard grows
I love her deeply, she'll never know

I once believed she'd bleed me my love,
but she left it cold in her veins
I once thought she'd drown in my springs,
but she made ice of my rains

The bark is frozen in Shiver-Shock Meadow
The deer are dead, yet taunting me
Lightning kicks bones out of the billows
My love is a curse which no one can see
I'm trapped outside of my heart within hers,
without any words to support her stay
If I can't find the trail of our love,
I'll die in these woods as she walks away

There is a man-child in mourning; awake with but a dream. Between panic and a bloody
pulse, he runs; looking for a way into that garden which grows his lover. Yet, at the same
time, he's hoping to escape any memory of her; crying out for the will to read a raven's
mind, for it knows the way. But he just gets colder, as does the forest he's scrambling
about. Just as he's giving up on ever finding any path leading anywhere, he spots a
clearing, housing a weathered castle at its core. Walking upon its gates, he spots a sign
which begs its readers for magic words. So he takes a cold breath, and says all that he can
still manage to manage, "I need only to know that she's still alive tonight; tell her I love
her, and die holding her hand." The walls begin to shake. The sun cuts itself free, and
blows them over; revealing his lost love with tears staining her cheeks. Her roses are
cold, but she's so very ready to have another know their scent.
She lifts her heavy head, and heaves the hearty lines,
"My love's forever been yours, and you are forever my love."

Shiver-Shock Meadow now holds no captives
Its visitors are cozy, and discovering color
The man finally understands that good love isn't suffered
He had to face the long season to fathom what would survive
And she wasn't haunting him;
she was waiting

Riddle of the Wind

Did you ever wake up in the moonlight,
and not see the moon,
then fall out of bed,
stand up in the closet,
missing a sock,
holding a toothbrush;
screaming, "Don't eat the brisket,
it's full of hiccups!" as those friggin' crickets
tune blades of grass?
...
It's maddening, you can be sure
And, betrayed by trust, I am haunted
Does that imply I believe in ghosts?
Riddle me this, and roll me away

To Help You Understand What I Don't

I've often wondered what goes through your head
when people assume we're together,
in spite of our just being friends
And I've fallen asleep questioning
if you defend this friend when he's not around,
and doesn't quite live up to your virtues
It's difficult for me to accept your simple reasons
for loving me like you do,
so I seem to be slowly convincing myself that you don't;
mostly my head though, as my heart looks on and laughs
Truth be told, I know better than to doubt you,
for you watched me fall over other girls
before I even knew you were alive
And, now that the tables have turned,
I'm not sure what you see or what I should feel
Although I know these questions have answers,
I wish you'd give them ahead of me asking

73

A Fallacy of Myth

The innate fascination of a moving
freezer burn
A creature which fears itself
Rumored to be a rumor;
too much of a marvel
for the eyes to take in
Last in line for realization,
but concluded by the K of nights
Left undisturbed in a dormant dwelling,
where fire is as dead as I am
to your mind;
yet we both know you'd love to believe
I am...
A butterfly's second cousin,
but not quite as pretty
Ancient and breathless;
almost forgotten

...

Hope for Your Heart

Her first word was Daddy,
though you tried to explain
it would only be Mommy;
of him, you're ashamed
"Where's my Father?" she asks
at the prying age of five
Hard to face the girl and admit,
"I'm not sure he's alive."
She deserves what's not there,
but that's not your fault
If you live for the ocean,
you can't scorn the salt
Keep right on moving
from new day to next night
She may have her questions,
and there will be some fights,
but that little girl loves you
more than one should allow
So, just be a mother
Don't give up on her now
For there's a point in time
when we all lose our way,
but we pick ourselves up,
and we learn to say,
"I'll make a life of my time.
Yes, I'm going to live.
I will let the past go,
and learn how to forgive;
because I've got reasons
to make these dreams come true."
So never doubt when in darkness
that you'll get through

The Girl Is a Ghost

She said she could tell from the moment we met
that I'd be the one to take everything she had;
everything,
from her virginity to her heart
And as autumn spun that stunning web in her mouth,
I refused to take my eyes off of it

She lit a joint, but retained her innocence
She blew the smoke in my eyes, and kissed me
before I could clearly see it coming
We got high, and I went down;
making a reality of her premonition

Yet as soon as I'd taken her where she'd always wanted to go,
she began to cry, slow in the fade
Reaching for my face with hands which couldn't feel
Trying to kiss with lips like a fog
And with the breeze went the last remnants of her apparition;
leaving only her tears on the ground

The morning's sunlight held a cruel bag of realization in its birth
As I opened my mind to the pillow in my arms
and the sleep still in my eyes,
the truth was far too apparent

I'd been dreaming again;
dreaming about the one I'm too afraid to hold with words
(I truly believe they don't always exist in her presence)
The one who's no longer within my spectrum of love
The one who's always seemed happiest without me

...The girl is a ghost...

And, in a dreamland that won't turn her away,
I'm her god

Jack-O-Lantern

Treated by tricksters
on roads blackened by subtlety's supple moontan;
we are gathering
And the shades, they know the game's begun
So they rasp, at last, the gasp of All Hallows;
let unfold their hold on the mystics and monsters
who just wish to roam these streets for sweets

Goodies covered with bows and white stockings
stand giddy upon the rock-beds;
unsure, but not undone
Untold stories open to suggestions
And the stars, they know that twilight is theirs
So they sugar these blossoms with wishful thinking;
blanket the cold grown old in warm flesh
Thus welcome the soft vampires of our desires,
who know how to bleed us
back into (and unto) comfort

Cozy as all fright should be, we fall
And by morning the pumpkins are void of this night
which gave way to a light
that remains the candy in our mask-less mouths

CHAPTER SEVEN

-*Verbatim*-

Kindergarten Heart

...

Assorted Mumbles

...

Learning to Fall

...

Drowned Beside Freedom,
Entranced Among Cinders

...

Pillow Talk

...

Dark Lightning

...

Everything Comes Down

...

Vertical Syllables

...

Covered In Your Tears

...

Bubbly, Bedbug-Less Dreamscapes

...

Lullaby of the Night

...

Death to the Simpleton

Kindergarten Heart

The last year I spent in those apartments
we could rap Mary Poppins tunes, but little more
We were still eating cold bologna and ketchup sandwiches,
and the little world around us was so amazingly vast
Ceiling fans were almost as tall as the sky,
and the rain never kept us inside;
though I'm still afraid I'll be struck by the lightning
...
In those days I had heroes,
a full moon or a Friday which fell on the 13th were haunting,
and my feet never hurt;
unless I did something foolish, like step on a nail
...
One day, in that field which now looks so dead,
I stood a good three feet high in the grass
watching the wind move blades of it around my waist;
like I was swimming in the earth
as hot air balloons hovered jealously in the distance
But now I see nothing more than sun,
shielding my eyes from what you'd think
would be clearly evident;
there's nothing left up there to see
...
Once upon a better time
we threw cats over second story railings,
just to watch them land on their feet
(even now, that puzzles me)
We swam all summer, and never learned how to drown
With a simpler idol;
the familiar blended scent of sun-block and chlorine
...
But if the world really has made me colder,
I think it must know it made a mistake
Why else would there be so much sun upon us...
making mid-winter this warm?

Assorted Mumbles

...At times I find myself avoiding
the right kind of people,
tor fear they may reveal a vulgar truth
when it's too late to walk away
· (as though people who are
openly ugly from the start are any better)
...I'm a fool that queens want to make a king,
simply because I don't ignore my emotions
But I'll end up letting all of them down
For, though it's plain enough to me,
some fail to fathom that
we have to let everyone down
Yet I still imply that I deserve a crown
...I hate being so intimate with insecurity
It doesn't feel like I'm the one that's choosing
my friends and would-be lovers
It always seems to be
me as the scared and undeserving introvert,
waiting to find their approval
(perhaps a superior word would be tolerance)
...It's so easy to think you're fearless,
then the butterflies begin to burn,
and you're suddenly relieved
of those words you'd recited for days;
the questions you knew you wanted to ask
And you're altogether naked once again

Learning to Fall

Do I believe in a god?
I long to
So you couldn't really call me a believer
Because if there is a god,
it's very lonely
And I don't feel a need to die
to find this so-called Heaven
For the angels are already here with me,
and I know them all by name

Drowned Beside Freedom,
Entranced Among Cinders

so Pamper that last tiny inkling of sleep
the Endless consumption of time?
and Never let go of the rain
Can you prove that I'm without
for Intricate layers of faith
this Lament is like euphoric waiting...

Pillow Talk

I still pretend I'm holding you close
when I'm all alone in my bed,
listening to the raindrops battle the roof;
letting me just be right where I am
But how long can a dream
really keep one awake?
If I were in love, I'd breathe it
Were I without love, I'd seek it
But I'm all, and I'm none;
crippled now, next to your memory
And there's not a whole hell of a lot I can keep
saying about how I'm getting along without you
I mean, what does it change?
You never cared about me to begin with
And maybe I've already got the best of you
Maybe you're only good for fantasy
Maybe I'm the lucky one,
and it's you who's missing out
After all,
years from now,
you'll only know what life was like
without me

Dark Lightning

Out of the sky they came,
like fallen angels falling
Stood, unstirred in the moonlight;
staring with deep black eyes
They stayed focused on my fear,
then simply shot off, calling;
leaving me amid the darkness
with nothing but their cries

And their eyes haunt me now;
that ever-intense dissidence
Never blinking, nothing like it,
or has ever been there since

As I stand (as I said) alone,
I wonder where they are
I am bathed in moonbeams,
but the world's wrapped in blankets of shade
Years don't kill those images;
nearer now than can be far
And every corner contains a gaze
which doesn't seem to want to fade

And their eyes haunt me still;
that always-intense dissidence
Never blinking, nothing like it,
or has yet to be there since

Were my eyes engaged in games,
or were they as real as I have feared;
these beings which fell through moonlight,
took my eyes, and then disappeared?

Everything Comes Down

The thunder will never harm you,
your mind will never be flawless,
and love will never win the war

Everything is futile, one way or another
For you will die, one way or another
Youthful beauty will fade,
one way or another
Yet (and still)...
hearts which don't exist hold on

Peace will never keep you sane,
faith will never make you superior,
and you won't find all you're looking for

I offend myself,
but I had no angels
And this goes to show
that you can't fully heal the world;
for every giving person
is but helping another fall faster

Vertical Syllables

May hearts,
yearning to wish;
strumming chords in lone dreams
Thoughtfully hoping to become
something...

In this
Netherland of
trust, awaiting a friend,
harmony cries out to us all;
enticed...

Must we
offer ourselves
openly to unknown
nothing, and the dark eyes of the
dauntless?

Let us
infiltrate the
glistening sounds of our
heartstrings, until we kowtow to
these dreams!

Covered In Your Tears

Anger-riddled coals are dimming
below the snows
(which choke our air visible)
as you bury your head in my arms;
warming your body against mine
Two weathered wishers in one calming coat

My fingers run the length of your spine;
entwined with the snowflakes
as they land upon us
And every deity we're unsure of
must covet the brilliance we exchange

No words exhaled; none necessary
You lift your eyes to find my gaze
(once lost in the white, but since lost in you)
Crying, I am
overjoyed to be as I've become;
covered in your tears,
and covered in the love
so easily evident within them

Suddenly everything I thought I was dying for
has given me many new reasons to live

Bubbly, Bedbug-Less Dreamscapes

I tend to be narcissistic in certain types of moonlight,
because I love what I love, and it's all part of me
I'm a brother to my sisters,
because everyone deserves to know when they're needed
I like musicals, of all things;
not because I believe it's what a woman wants,
but because no one is safe when they're no longer childish
I still think love will find me again,
because the unexpected kindnesses I'm handed,
day after day, are lending the hope
that's building this bridge
back to a heart I thought I'd drowned
I want people to know that,
while my confidence may be pessimistic, I'm not
We need to understand that,
even though those greener pastures will always exist,
someday someone is likely to adore us
for reasons which aren't immediately apparent
For instance; I don't like kittens, but I adore people who do
I like sitting in the dark,
listening to the Counting Crows,
but I'd prefer not doing it alone
I'd be lying out under the sky,
just anticipating the contribution of a shooting star,
were it not that I was under my ceiling thinking this over;
dreaming up the belief in a thought
which implies that there's a love somewhere
to revoke this conviction
I've sentenced my own heart to
A love to open the door, lull me out,
and help me prove what a brother knows

Lullaby of the Night

Treading the night-trail,
floating in ozone;
my fingertips caught in the stars

Where the songbird still twitters
amidst the cold;
slumber-rocking the eye of Heaven,
fast asleep upon my dream

I hemorrhage absolution
on a lagging nightmare;
kindle concrete clouds
in a thicket of shades,
as I roam...

Death to the Simpleton

Simple creatures, convinced of our complexity;
taught to hide, and born to die
So I write, for I'm
too weak to step outside the lines

CHAPTER EIGHT
-*Kiss the Rain*-

Empathy, I Give Myself

...

Echoes of Fallen Tears

...

We Called Her Moonlight

...

Untitled Love

...

Perfect

...

How She Dulls My Sunset

...

Conspiracy of the Past to Break Me

...

For the Weary Snowflake

...

Gubblebum

...

Friends without Friends

...

I Still Believe in Unicorns

...

Innocence Ease

Empathy, I Give Myself

If I'm second best, never second-guess
what you do in the world
Of course I'm upset,
but you left before asking
It takes more out of me
than a tear could tell you
So I no longer cry,
for my own sake

Echoes of Fallen Tears

This is the only way left for me to let you know
what you needed to know all along;
I love you
And it's only the parts of my heart
that are still worth having
which always will
And, having said it,
knowing no apology will ever be enough,
I'll mumble a goodbye you'll never hear,
and just pray that this helps me to let you go

We Called Her Moonlight

It was two a.m. that desolate night,
when she found the path to our site
And we assumed she was moonlight

The day had been sweet with snow;
filled with a bliss we no longer know
But night brought fear we'd never let go

One of our party had left at dawn;
to a funeral this acquaintance had gone,
returning before the eve was upon

Late upstairs we began to fight
Much later downstairs we talked, despite
how the waters of dread spun satellites

She appeared like the dusk's burnt desire,
and hovered amidst the trees like white fire;
the look on her face was of morbid dire

We struck like lightning back to bed,
for nothing alive ever looked so dead,
with a merciless thirst which had to be fed

She reached the window, and disappeared
Yet something existed which still we feared;
though the dark was once more, lone and cleared

Then *he* began to shout and moan;
cry, he screamed, and sigh, he groaned
She was still there, we weren't alone

He attended the funeral, you see
This spirit for him; final destiny;
the lay ghost, white flames, a soul from the trees

It was two a.m. that desolate night,
when she found herself in our sight
And we still call her moonlight

Untitled Love

Sometimes I lose sight of who you really were;
the sound of your voice,
the color of your eyes,
pretty much anything that meant
everything to me about you
Sometimes I turn to look back,
and try finding the misplaced pieces of myself,
but memories of you clutter the path I've traveled
It's not a bad thing for me to realize
you're the missing link in this chain
Do you (in the vicinity of your now-dead mind)
recall the kitten we caught on the side of the road?
You let me keep it,
and never has a gift meant half as much
I always assumed that cat
would be the first of us to go
How much did it cost a heart
to care as much as yours?
I never felt shame in your presence,
and I never got the chance to feel guilt
You were my standards for forgiveness and warmth
But will I ever hear you laugh again,
or see you shine as bright?
Am I bound to feel comfort again in those arms,
such as I did when you were living?
None can say, and so I'm left asking:
How much does it cost a heart
to care as much as yours?

Perfect

The skies paint emotions, and reflect them onto ocean waves,
which wash ashore with the tide
Then they're carried by the wind through the trees,
'til they find your face, and there they hide

Today the woods were a whisper of,
"Love is born in the breeze."
But will you spread your wings and fly?

I wish that here you might end up,
so that this heart could know ease,
long before the winds die

For in my mind you walk on water
In my mind you're asleep on the moon
In this mind you're frozen beautifully
Break away, and soothe me soon

The fire in your eyes melts me whole, and I flow
like pouring rain through your gentle fingers
The pigment of your skin, like carnations in bloom,
gets caught in my mind, and left to linger

You sip iced tea, then smile;
stars dancing in your eyes
I send these wishes in deep

So send your wishes my way;
all of those unheard cries
Don't leave our adoration to weep

For in my life you live the lead;
the only reason that I survive
Let your eyes breathe hope into me
Let your lips keep me alive

Because we could make this thing between us perfect,
if you'll just say more than you do

How She Dulls My Sunset

There's only one pair
of eyes in the world
that have truly shaken my core,
but they didn't carry more
than my name
Truly love at first sight
'neath the autumn dawn's light,
but beyond what I saw
lay a trail too fearful to take;
so I didn't
Now I have to live with that,
until I find a way to get back to her
And I've never been good
with possibilities

Conspiracy of the Past to Break Me

Putting memories in boxes gets old
I want you back in my life,
telling me I'm too serious
Because all I have left are pictures of you
rolling your eyes at me,
and your goofy signature
on pieces of pink notebook paper
And, like I said, it gets old

For the Weary Snowflake

Your eyes remind me of cold days in the rain,
where no one could see my tears through the downpour
Your eyes are icy angels, hopelessly blue
And it sickens me to know that I never noticed them
before they started becoming so much like mine
I can't quit thinking that I helped drive them there;
even though our circumstances
were fucked from the get-go
Still, I let you spare me of the details
I've been such a pathetic imitation of a friend

And there lays the fault steadily hanging in my mind;
still haunting that pretty face of yours
each time it comes my way

I just hope you know how much I love you
And I hope to find the moment I can tell you myself
that, even if you never create an excuse
which lets you kick in my door
(if you never need me to need you),
I'll always be here; waiting to catch your tears
in the event you want me there when they fall
That's what I'm hoping you want
more than anything else in your world
It may be asking too much,
but, even though you're icy, you'll always be an angel
to me

Gubblebum

There was never a day
when babies were babies
that she didn't suck her thumb

And rarely a moment
when she smiled or talked
that you'd miss her gubblebum

She'd throw her fits,
and throw off her clothes
She'd always eat a little dirt

She'd trip and fall
just to limp to your side,
and tell you it didn't hurt

But innocence is precious
Exception, she's not
She's far too endearing to be dumb

So when she fails a lesson
life is handing her,
try giving more gubblebum

Friends without Friends

Lina cries more than she lets on
Her heart speaks through her eyes,
and you'll never hear it over the phone
So, we haven't spoken in some time
But I still want to give her hope,
and be there to hold her
when she doesn't realize
it's what she needs
Sadly, she's never known the me she needs,
for I too am undeniably shattered
And I can't summarize
when it comes to love
I need a day like today, alone with her,
to soothe her lullabies to sleep
Because I'm still a sleepless dreamer,
waiting
And I can't call this living;
going without the one person
who never failed to make me feel alive
It continues to ring true
Yes, I do
miss that girl

I Still Believe in Unicorns

The splendor in every little thing
is slowly slipping away from me,
and all newness in the day
bares likeness to fading memories

My visions are growing grayer
My pulse is getting colder
My faith is basically gone

But, as the seasons lose their flavor,
I must remember I've forgotten

I had dreams
I've still got dreams
And this war isn't over until I'm smiling again

So, bring on your minions,
but (I warn you now) they'll lose

Because this is my fight

And dreamers don't simply stop dreaming

No, it's not about the glory
It's not about the pride
It's about overcoming
what my fears have denied

And, damnitt all, I will

Innocence Ease

I've always been a crier,
except for all those times that I wanted to cry the most
And every sign I see says crying is not an option,
but I'm doing it now, so I suppose it must be

Damn this heartless world

All I've done for weeks is think about finally seeing you again;
drowning in your four-second hug
Knowing all that I'd remember about this night
is everything I still adore about you
How your company never gets old;
never wears away its welcome
How you just keep looking better to me

We've got too much in common
to wither or weather away in silence;
letting the world undo what I've tried so hard to solidify
But you don't miss me at all, do you?
Or are you just afraid that I don't care?
I'm sure it's difficult;
trying to find what I hide so well

So, I'm reassuring you now,
knowing I should have been saying this all along:
If your bed is ever not warm enough to keep you safe and secure
(if your pillows can't dry all those tears),
I could be the one you keep beside you
You can always turn to me,
because you're almost everything that I now love about my life
I'll never deny it,
and I'll never run

CHAPTER NINE
-*Walter Mitty's Rebuttal*-

Pieces of Clouds

...

More of What I Know to Be True

...

Ragdoll Curtain Call

...

The Last Days of Love

...

Laundering Dirt

...

How He Holds Her

...

Short of Sweet

...

A. B. See?

...

Embers

...

Sweet Depression

...

Emoness

...

Beyond the Encore

Pieces of Clouds

Most memories look best
in black and white
Most women look best
when they suggest they're at their worst
Few things are as timeless
as yesterdays can be,
but they're infinite in their endurance
And the only way to move forward
is to keep on looking back

More of What I Know to Be True

Peace!
To the countries of the world,
I preach it
But no one's ever gonna learn,
because nobody will
teach it

Ragdoll Curtain Call

The lights bore a princess from a golden rainbow,
and she spouts prose like a demon
with a key to the doors of Avalon
She gives justice to the words
which our gods bleed through her lips
And she dances with every ghost on the floor

The mortals give way to whimpers and tears;
drowned amongst their own emotion,
like a dying river feeding the skies

Her aura glows like a bonfire
that's a shade or two above her head,
as the last line flies from her zenith
to be devoured by enlightened minds

And finally... the silence

They disband;
departing from the props adorning a deserted stage
And the ghosts of that night are still
dancing within the moment;
dancing the memory to death,
'til it is, forever, part of their hearts

The Last Days of Love

The thought turned to me,
and echoed its way to words
"She'll stop calling you home today."

My mouth spit through me;
a resignation tendered
"Cry." The word said, then obeyed

Far through the night, I fled
into the darkness; aware
Though I never left this room

Absconding from my dread
Purging the shadow's stare
of torrentially gloomy doom

But she found me, and pulled me to her
Warring within my fear;
she knelt, and took my hands

I said, "You need love me no longer.
For in spite of the years,
we'll fall through the other like sands."

She quietly wiped my tears away,
then smiled at me with concern;
hoping her words would be enough

"We're more now than in any yesterday.
It may take you a lifetime to learn,
but there is no end to any love."

The last days of love don't exist
Break my heart, yet it may reminisce
for the sake of another's love

Laundered Dirt

Gnawing at my cuticles;
trying to fill the hole
between us and them, her and him,
and lives we used to know
But I can't talk about these thoughts
without the thoughts that brought 'em
Just a boy without a toy;
dumb 'cause no one taught him

Spiders, insiders, lighters and pain
Clothes left damp without the rain

Disdain and such, we complain too much,
but at least we do it well
Still believing we're headed for Heaven,
for our lives have been pure Hell
But I kind of like having little to love,
so I'm gonna love even less
For if I can ignore just a little bit more,
I may lose faith in happiness
And should I dare to choose to care,
I'd discern that I haven't been blest

Such is the life going nowhere

How He Holds Her

If you ever see her out after sunset,
talking her tears to the moon,
you too may begin to believe
in breath beyond departure
For there's a father up there somewhere
who still considers her to be his home,
and listens to everything she has to say;
proud of the woman she struggles to be
(one ruled by her heart,
and rarely supported with peace of mind)
No, it's not as easy as she makes it look
And sometimes,
when there's nothing else left to smile about,
and these talks are all she can count on,
she'll hear the familiar echo of his jokes
retold in her memories;
reminding her that it will all be okay

...

Now that Daddy's on the moon,
her nights are never as lonely as they could be,
and there are no more reasons to fear the dark

Short of Sweet

You say I'm soft like you wish I weren't-wasn't,
then chase that same fool who can't and doesn't
love anything more than your ass
You fish for compliments, and catch his rejection,
Because I'm not worthy of your hooks or affection
But I can't just let this pass
...
So, if you're seeking a panic to comfort,
just know I'd give you that chance

A. B. See?

I can't sit here in the dark,
and tell you I'm not shaking
I won't deny the frightened tears
you hear in my voice
I can't tell you I love you, though I know that I do
Nobody left me a choice

I feel you
I know you
I don't want to lose you,
but how do you make a heart believe it deserves?

Embers

Let's start a conversation that's never going to end
Just hug me, hold me, and refuse to let go
Because if you turn to leave me now,
I never will get over this
It's how good you always manage to smell,
the way you yawn with your hands in your hair,
and how my heart dreams when watching you sleep
Every detail that makes this necessary
will linger inside of me, yearning to have you back

I still don't understand why you want to walk away

So just stay with me tonight,
and stop crying long enough to tell me what's wrong
Bleed yourself to me,
and by the time the dawn arrives
we'll both be okay again
Then maybe you'll be able to believe me
a little more often when I tell you
that loving you isn't enough

Sweet Depression

I wish I could drown beautifully,
but when the hope is gone
I still want to believe

I cry for no reason;
convincing myself that it's better this way,
but the truth is I'm blind to any reason

Grace, I'm sinking,
and I'm not sure an afterlife awaits

I miss every little detail of happiness
It's a shame the rain can't talk back,
for it's the only friend I've got

The clocks are ticking without their hands,
corruption is under my fingernails,
and the water is so deep

Grace, I'm breathing,
but I'm never sure that afterlife awaits

Emoness

You don't know whom, and you don't know why,
but you were taken as a child
from your perch of simple purity
to tears upon the stars

But in the color red
(blind eyes from inanimate photos)
you're a dust-free recollection,
and the first shy breath I ever took

So to the petrified sadness you are,
I offer the chance to be
a vital, heated moan;
a quivering bashfulness

I'll give you a heartbeat;
take you up and out
to a moon-melting summit,
where another star may dry your tears
...
And I'll hold you until the sun has set again

Beyond the Encore

Now digging deep
in the darkness
for some form of
inspiration,
but all I've got left is a pen in hand
So, I think I'll put it away
for a while,
and face the open road
on the other side of this door

113

THE EXPERIENCE DOESN'T END HERE

Complete your collection of The Secret Me books today
by purchasing any of the following online:

The Secret Me: A Biased Perspective

The Secret Me: A Companion's Relic

The Secret Me: A Companion's Relic (naming edition)

The Secret Me: A Couch Potato's Take (table game edition)

The Secret Me: A Couch Potato's Take (television edition)

The Secret Me: A Couch Potato's Take (video game edition)

The Secret Me: A Fantasy Manifesto

The Secret Me: A Film Fanatic's Record

The Secret Me: A Harry Potter Examination

The Secret Me: A List Lover's Keepsake

The Secret Me: A Music Enthusiast's Diary (volume one)

The Secret Me: A Music Enthusiast's Diary (volume two)

The Secret Me: A Music Enthusiast's Diary (unguided edition)

The Secret Me: A Questionnaire Journal

The Secret Me: A Questionnaire Journal 2

The Secret Me: A Questionnaire Journal for Teens

The Secret Me: A Rated Survey

The Secret Me: A Rated Survey 2

The Secret Me: A Shared Life Log (volume one)

The Secret Me: A Shared Life Log (volume two)

Most every book in the series can be obtained online for under $10!
They ship fast, and often free, from the world's
most trusted book source.

Newly available:

11:36

The first recorded collection of original songs by Shane Windham.
Accessible through nearly every major digital music retailer.
www.shanewindham.com/music

Poetry collections:

Thought-Box

"Remind her that she's beautiful, until she can see how beautiful she is."

Ink and Emotion

"Blanket the cold grown old in warm flesh."

Nevermore Forevermore

"Our love is still in the making."

Fancy Gravity

"Your smile alone is worth living for."

The Shallow Waters of Heaven

Books 1-4 of Shane's poetic works bound in a single hardback anthology.

Emotional Mythologies

"I write because your heart needs a hero."

Majestria

"There's no forgetting diamonds once you've worn them."

POETiCA

"You're a pen. The world is paper."

The Astrals

"Whatever makes you ache."

The Safe Side of Hell

Books 5-8 of Shane's poetic works bound in a single hardback anthology.

81 Miles: Best Loved Poems

Experience the most cherished writings of Shane Windham's career.

Own them all on the Kindle for a fraction of the cost.

Peruse official merchandise by visiting:

www.shanewindham.com/merch

Available now online:

SHANE WINDHAM'S GAMES

Great for parties, small gatherings, or even as gifts.
Try a game or two for free today by visiting:
www.shanewindham.com/games

Games by Shane Windham:

Diecraft
A Minecraft inspired role-playing game.

Fantasy Cardball
A unique take on American fantasy football.

Guess-Heads
A mystery word game of deduction in 20 questions or less.

Humans Against Everything
Social party games for apes that read.

The Mean Scene
A drinking game of discrimination, for better or worse.

PegNote
A deck of varied music guessing games.

Pinions
A friendly fiasco of judgmental proportions.

Round Robbin'
An eclectic game of categorical quandaries.

Table Games
More than 50 original games using cards, dice and dominoes.

Treasure Caves
An objective based race to find the rarest of riches.

TSM: Biased
An official card game version of 'The Secret Me: A Biased Perspective'.

Wicked Company
A Halloween inspired card game about friendship, imagination… and murder.

Learn more about the author by visiting:

www.shanewindham.com

26919510R00074

Printed in Great Britain
by Amazon